as

saw

HERBERT HOOVER

May 26, 1929 — *How Will Hoover Go Down in History?*

as

saw

HERBERT HOOVER

by JAY N. DARLING

as edited by
JOHN M. HENRY

with Introduction by
Timothy Walch

IOWA STATE UNIVERSITY PRESS / AMES

Jay N. Darling was an editorial cartoonist whose artwork appeared daily on the front page of the *Des Moines Register* between 1906 and 1949. For nearly three decades his cartoons were syndicated to 135 newspapers across the country. Darling twice received the Pulitzer Prize for editorial cartooning—in 1924 and again in 1943.

Timothy Walch is director of the Herbert Hoover Presidential Library in West Branch, Iowa. He is a member of the Society of American Archivists, the U.S. Catholic Historical Society, and the Organization of American Historians.

© 1996 Iowa State University Press, Ames, Iowa 50014; © 1954 John M. Henry, *As Ding Saw Hoover*

The Ding Darling cartoons are reprinted herein, courtesy of the J. N. "Ding" Darling Foundation.

♾ Printed on acid-free paper in the United States of America

First Iowa Heritage Collection edition, 1996

Library of Congress Cataloging-in-Publication Data

Darling, Jay N. (Jay Norwood), 1876–1962.
    As Ding saw Herbert Hoover / by Jay N. Darling as edited by John M. Henry; with introduction by Timothy Walch.—1st Iowa heritage collection ed.
      p. cm.—(Iowa heritage collection)
    ISBN 0-8138-2343-9 (alk. paper)
    1. Hoover, Herbert, 1874–1964—Caricatures and cartoons. 2. United States—Politics and government—1929–1933—Caricatures and cartoons. 3. Political satire, American. 4. American wit and humor, Pictorial. I. Henry, John M. II. Title. III. Series.
E802.D37   1996
973.91'6'0207—dc20   95-46890

Library of Congress number for *As Ding Saw Hoover*: 54-11723

Cartoons and Commentary

Part IV — President

Part V — Post-Presidential Years

Introduction

JAY DARLING AND HERBERT HOOVER: THE STORY OF A FRIENDSHIP

J AY DARLING was a Hoover man through and through. "Ding," as he was known to most of his friends, remembered meeting the future president at a European relief rally in Des Moines during World War I. Ding had gone to the rally as an editorial cartoonist to get a personal look at the man who was feeding Europe, a man who Darling had found difficult to capture on paper. At a brief introduction following the rally, Hoover acknowledged Ding and told him his cartoons "had been a great help" to the food relief effort.

That brief encounter was the beginning of a friendship that lasted until Ding's death in 1962. They corresponded regularly during the 1920s, with Ding complimenting Hoover on various speeches or Department of Commerce initiatives and Hoover praising Ding for his cartoons and sending him copies of various books and speeches. Their contact during most of the decade was casual and incidental.

When Hoover became president, however, the relationship changed somewhat. Ding took on the role of an unofficial advisor to the president. He recommended and evaluated potential presidential appointments and provided advice on a range of issues, including home building, farm mortgages, veterans' hospitals, and the Reconstruction Finance Corporation.

Ding's direct contact with Hoover increased during the presidency and on at least three occasions, the Darlings were overnight guests at the White House. Certainly the first visit made quite an impact and Hoover received a personalized cartoon of the Darling family "returning to Earth." More important, that visit laid the foundation for regular visits between these two men who shared a political philosophy and a passion for fishing.

In fact, they fished together on a number of occasions. First at Camp Rapidan, where they also enjoyed giving the slip to naive secret service agents assigned to protect them. "Those week-end trips," remembered Ding years later, "were the only hours when I saw Herbert Hoover, as President, do anything but work."

Their friendship deepened in the years after the presidency. Overwhelmed with appeals for financial aid in the months after he left Washington, Hoover asked Ding to investigate some of the neediest cases. This Darling did with great satisfaction and success; his reward was a fishing trip with the former president in October 1933.

But the two men shared more than fishing. In the early months of 1934, as Hoover was finishing his book *The Challenge to Liberty*, Darling spent six weeks in Washington working on a federal program for wildlife restoration. "It was an interesting experience," Darling wrote to Hoover on February 24, "and I got a pretty good glimpse into the inside working of the Administration."

JULY 5, 1929—Ding Darling and his family were honored with a personal invitation to visit President Hoover at the White House on June 28, 1929. It was a heady experience for all the Darlings, and Ding captured the moment in this "thank-you" cartoon sent to the president on the fifth of July.

Such a comment whetted Hoover's interest. "There seems to be a fairly definite philosophic pattern underlying the New Deal," Hoover wrote on March 1. "I am wondering what your own reaction is as to its character and destination after you have soaked it up for two or three weeks in Washington."

Darling's response may have surprised the former president. "I am convinced that there is no pattern," Darling wrote. "As matters stand, I can only watch with tremulous apprehension the reckless speed with which we are traveling toward an undefined goal." Yet Darling was not quite ready to quit the government. "I see for myself a chance to do a job for conservation," he wrote. "If I wait until a change of administration it will be too late." Darling stayed on as chief of the Bureau of Biological Survey at the Department of Agriculture until 1935.

The friendship survived Ding's government service, which he saw on behalf of conservation, not in support of Franklin Roosevelt. Toward the end of his tenure at the Survey, Ding invited Hoover to his Des Moines home. "I could get quite a chuckle," he wrote to Hoover in May 1935, "out of the headline 'Herbert Hoover entertained by representative of the Roosevelt administration.'" Although Hoover was not able to visit, he did enjoy the joke.

Two years later, Hoover contacted Ding on behalf of the Huntington Library in Pasadena, California. The library staff had tried to reach Darling to obtain permission to use his drawings in a handbook, but to no avail. As a last resort, the director turned to Hoover, a member of the Huntington governing board, and the former president got the job done. "What do handbooks and libraries of knowledge matter," Ding cabled Hoover, "when fish are biting and government disintegrated. However, since you insist [I] have wired Huntington Library to do anything they darn please, just like Roosevelt."

The two men got together regularly at the annual Bohemian Grove encampments in the northern California woods. In fact, Hoover so enjoyed Ding's companionship at these events that he sponsored him for full membership in the club. On the sponsoring certificate, Hoover described Darling in longhand as "a great cartoonist—the greatest today. Fine companionable person."

But as much as Ding enjoyed the former president's company, he did not agree with him on everything. Differences of opinion became evident as Hoover spoke out on the problems of a lasting peace and the U.S. role in the war in Europe. "Can't you get the chief to pipe down for a while?" Ding wrote to their mutual friend, Mark Sullivan, in April 1941. "I know you can't. He is still the best American I know, but he is certainly ruining his chances to be used when the nation will need him most by his present ineffective tactics."

Three years later, however, Ding heralded Hoover's remarks at the opening session of the 1944 Republican national convention. "Your message tonight," Ding telegrammed, "was the most magnificent statement of American principles that has been uttered in my life time. My prayer is that the Republican Party may live up to it with pride and affection." In fact, Ding went so far as to make the speech the subject of his next editorial cartoon, which he entitled "New Dealers Didn't Like Hoover's Speech."

Over the next decade the two men saw each other occasionally and stayed in touch by letter. Ding sought out the former president's ideas on conservation and wrote to congratulate him on various speeches. When Hoover took up the cause of government reorganization for a second time in 1954, Darling wrote on behalf of the National Park Service and the environment. "I am always glad to have a word from you and to have your views," Hoover responded. "I will pass them on."

During the spring of 1954, the two men corresponded more frequently. The former president was to be honored in West Branch on August 10 on the occasion of his eightieth birthday. One of the birthday gifts would be the first edition of *As Ding Saw Hoover,* and the former president wanted to be sure that the author would be present at the occasion.

But Ding wasn't so sure he wanted to be there. "I find myself very much embarrassed by the emphasis they are giving to the cartoons I made during my acquaintance with you and the campaign," he wrote to Hoover on April 16. "They sent me a set of proofs and I blush at their inadequacy. I should have done a better job." But Ding agreed to be in West Branch nonetheless. The Chief had asked him to be there and he would comply with the request.

The August celebration went off without a hitch. Ding, however, was under the weather following a stay in the hospital in June. He did make the trip to West Branch and got his chance to meet with the former president, but only briefly on that hot August day.

Ding continued to write to Hoover throughout 1955. They commiserated over the possibility of the Corps of Engineers taking control of the nation's watersheds. They celebrated Ding's nomination to receive the Iowa Award, an honor that had gone to Hoover the previous year. Ding railed against the lack of interest in conservation projects shown by the Eisenhower administration, and Hoover asked about the fishing in Florida.

The letters became less frequent over the next few years. Ding congratulated the former president on his speech to the 1956 Republican national convention and in years to come sent other notes of gratitude and postcards from his travels. Hoover always responded with a note or one of his books or both.

By late 1961, Ding was in declining health. A stroke in mid December had disabled him and the former president sent a note of good cheer. "At this season," Hoover wrote, "life-long friends pass through one's mind. And those whose undeviating devotion over nearly forty years rise in the first rank. So this is just to record again my gratitude and to wish you a happier New Year." This brief note was better than medicine and Ding responded with a three-page letter of memories.

The winter of 1962 had the two men planning a fishing trip in Florida. Ding's spirit was willing, but chronic bronchitis slowed him down. "You'll hear from me definitely, one way or the other," he wrote Hoover on January 29. But the trip was not to be. Ding died of a heart ailment on February 12, 1962, ending a great friendship.

Ding's work lives on in books such as this one. It was the first volume in what has become a genre in historical publishing—editorial cartoon perspectives of the presidents. Similar volumes have been published on Franklin D. Roosevelt, Harry S Truman, and some of our more-recent presidents. Certainly, others will be published in the future.

These books make us smile, laugh, and even appreciate our presidents.

Yet this book is more than the first title on a shelf. This edition, *As Ding Saw Herbert Hoover,* is a testament to a friendship. Ding Darling was a Hoover man, just like dozens of other men who were devoted to "the Chief." These men worked with the former president, sharing the belief that one man can make a difference in this world. This book is, therefore, both a salute to Herbert Hoover and a tribute to Jay Darling. More than two decades after his death, Ding can still teach us a thing or two about his favorite president.

TIMOTHY WALCH
Herbert Hoover Presidential Library
August 10, 1995

My Association With Herbert Hoover

by Jay N. Darling

THERE WAS A TIME when all that most people knew about Herbert Hoover was what they had been reading recently in the papers. That was back in the early days of World War I when Hoover's name had suddenly become a byword as that of the man who was heading the Belgian Relief campaign, which followed the ruthless invasion of that peaceful nation by the German army. Belgium, the most densely populated country in Europe, had been crushed, its homes destroyed; the people were hungry and desperately in need of all the aid this country and her neigbbors could give them. Sympathy was not enough. The emergency called for a nationwide volunteer service of men and women, a quick-functioning organization, the collection of vast amounts of food and clothing, and solution of the difficult problem of transportation and distribution.

Mr. Hoover had reached Des Moines, Iowa, on a hurried tour of the country to speak in behalf of the cause and to solicit cooperation. The ballroom of the Fort Des Moines Hotel was packed to the doors by an audience that had been greatly impressed by his unemotional but factual appeal. When he had finished speaking I fell into the long line of folks eager to shake the speaker's hand.

I remember that I had a special objective in mind. The cartoonists of the country (I, among them) were having a terrible time trying to catch a likeness of this stranger who had suddenly captured the imagination of the public. I recall what a shock I got when I first saw Mr. Hoover that evening and realized that the cartoons I had been drawing had not the slightest resemblance to the man on the platform. My back seat in the auditorium didn't help me much. For my purpose I needed a close-up look at the man. (It didn't do me much good, for Hoover was the hardest subject to caricature I ever encountered. It is a wonder he ever tolerated me as a friend.) The newspaper cartoonists of the country never did succeed in putting into their caricatures either a good likeness or the amazing attributes of this man who was later to become President of the United States.

Hoover never had much of the glad-hand greeter in him, and as I neared the rostrum I noted that he was holding his head slightly bowed and seemed to be addressing most of his scarcely audible responses to his vest buttons — a habit which he has overcome only in recent years. I never knew a man so completely devoid of bombast. To my great surprise, when I was introduced he looked up sharply, fixed me with a penetrating eye and said, "You're not Jay Darling, are you?" When I admitted to the crime he said, "What are you doing here?" "I live here and draw pictures for the newspapers," I replied. His face broke into a smile as he said, "Yes, I know. You have been a great help." That was all. And I went on down the line.

It was a number of years before I saw him again but that brief meeting was the beginning of a generous friendship which lifted me out of my boots, and pained me as well when later the country crucified him for calamitous circumstances which were not of his making. Never once did I hear from him during the eight years which he served as Secretary of Commerce under Harding and Coolidge except indirectly, when I heard from some friend that he had mentioned a cartoon of mine which he liked. Not until he had been elected and inaugurated as President did I learn that he still remembered the cartoonist from Iowa in a personal way. One afternoon a call came through from the White House to my room in the Register and Tribune building. Could I come to Washington for a week-end visit? No, he had nothing particularly in mind but he'd like to know what I was thinking about.

From that time on invitations came intermittently, and I got the impression that the calls came when he got fed up with the yes-men around him and wanted conversation with a free-wheeler from the uninhibited Middle West. In fact I was told as much by Mark Sullivan, one of the great newspaper commentators of that day and a frequent visitor at the White House.

After I got over walking stiff-legged in such rarefied

atmosphere, in spite of the fact that there was nothing formal or stuffy about my reception, I began to enjoy the rich association. It was fun getting up to an early start on the day with a game of volleyball on the White House grounds and to breakfast with the members of his Kitchen Cabinet. Occasionally I was invited to fish with him at his Rapidan camp. There we together carried boulders to build leaky dams in the trout streams, wet up to our waists, and rode horseback — which he detested but endured for health's sake!

I got a great kick out of some early rides on horseback when he managed to shake the Secret Service agents whose business it was to protect him. He had hated horses because, at one period in his life, he had had to spend about four months of the year riding them while out on government geological and geodetic surveys. My friend's dislike of horses was summed up pretty well in a statement about them I've often heard him give: "I have often wondered if a mistake had not been made when the horse was created. Geologically there had been camels before the horse. Why was the horse not given the camel's tank and thus save watering him more than once a day? Centipedes had been made. Why not have given a horse six short legs and thus he would be nearer the ground and have a better gait? Fish scales had been invented long before. Why not have put scales on the horse instead of hair, so that he did not annoy you all the time fighting flies?"

But there was one aspect of these equestrian adventures which he enjoyed. While he was on friendly terms with the Secret Service men it irked him tremendously to have them constantly riding herd on him. Riding horseback enabled him to escape them occasionally.

I was with him one Sunday morning on a horseback ride when he escaped from the vigilant guards. We had slipped away on a narrow, unmarked trail and when we could no longer look back and see the horses of the Secret Service agents we hurried through the woods for a Forestry Service fire tower. There we dismounted, hid our horses in the woods, and climbed to the top of the forest warden's lookout, where President Hoover watched with glee the Secret Service men far below, spurring their horses about in search of their lost ward.

Those week-end trips to the Rapidan camp were the only hours when I ever saw Herbert Hoover, as President, do anything but work.

I learned much by being allowed, now and then, to sit in on discussions with the President's advisors. I recall Hoover's premonition of financial troubles ahead and the planning of measures to meet the contingencies long before the depression set in. Despite the intensity of his devotion to the problems of state, there was a delightful atmosphere in the Hoover household which, for me and the members of my family (who were occasionally included in the invitations), never failed to be enjoyable.

Some incidents which stand out in my recollection of those associations with Mr. Hoover, while not historically important, were significant in the interpretation of his many-sided personality and may account for some of the unexplained consequences which later developed.

The President apparently never could remember that I was deaf, and continued his habit of addressing his remarks to his vest buttons in a voice so low that I frequently made a bad guess on what he was saying, and thought he was talking about pajamas when he was referring to Panama. My replies must have puzzled him at times. It was the only thoughtless trait I ever noted in his personal relationships. In a small group his conversation sparkled with humor and interest. I hated to miss any of it, so after many protests (which were seconded by Mrs. Hoover and the rest of his family) I canvassed the antique stores in search of an old-fashioned ear trumpet and found a collapsible instrument of ancient vintage which opened to a full ten inches. At the next opportunity I pulled this ear trumpet out to its full length and with ostentation aimed it at him and held it to my ear. I thought the "gentle hint" might do some good. But I don't believe he even noticed it. At least his low voice continued.

It was with secret elation that a few years ago I noticed him wearing, on occasions, a hearing aid. But even this has not completely cured him of what Mrs. Hoover often called his "awful habit." Mrs. Hoover did, however, occasionally persuade him to raise his voice while I was there. Only she could do it.

President Hoover never could adjust himself to the custom of being top man around the White House, and protested violently when the ushers held everyone else back — even the ladies — so the President of the United States might be first in or out of a White House elevator, or the first to enter or leave the dining room.

He ordered his complex days without seeming effort. The White House guests were always graciously kept busy but there was never any allowance made for negligence in the household activities. Punctuality was expected. When in Washington the President attended church with regularity and the President's family and any guests were always welcome to accompany him to church. The White House car and Mr. Hoover always appeared simultaneously at the carriage entrance and on the dot of the appointed time. Not a moment was wasted. Any laggards were left behind, with Mr. Hoover's gentle admonition, "We go to church on time or we don't go at all."

Hoover was at his best when fishing and he was an expert with the fly rod. When wading a trout stream he got complete relaxation for, said he, "There are only two times when a fellow can be free from all interruptions. One is at prayer and the other when stalking a wary trout." On the few occasions when he took me fishing with him, all visiting ceased as we reached the stream. He went one direction and I the other and I wouldn't see him again until the appointed hour to meet for grub.

His appetite was wonderfully persistent and omnivorous. Mealtime was always an occasion for good food, accompanied by good talk. If it hadn't been for Dr. Boone's watchfulness, Mr. Hoover would have had considerable difficulty with his waistcoat. I never knew him to have a physical complaint.

It was a common saying that Hoover had everything excepting a flair for politics. He had a strong distaste for superficial glad-handing and back-slapping, but there never was a question of his deep human sympathies — Belgium and the starving children of Russia provide adequate proof of that. But in all the years I have known him I have never heard out of him an ecstatic whoop in victory or a whimper in defeat and his self-effacing gesture of greeting, a limp lift of the hand, has been described by a friend as "a flag at half-mast on a windless day."

After the violent political eruption that retired him from the Presidency, I shared with him two incidences which illustrate the extremes of his reaction to fellow humans, and his unawareness of the political significance of his actions. I write of these with hesitancy lest I offend him, but I feel they may help some to interpret better the personality of the greatest man I have ever known.

A short time after his return to his home in Palo Alto, California, he wired to ask me to join him for a few days' fishing at his modest fishing camp on the Rogue River. We got an early start and drove north from his home along the scenic coastal highway of California, which landed us for an overnight stop in the heart of the Redwood forest. The second day, equally enjoyable and full of good chatter, took us across the border to Oregon where we stopped in a small town for a supply of camp groceries. Apparently fearing that someone might make a fuss over him if he were recognized, he pulled his head down into his collar and shaded his face under his hat brim — a reflection of that great modesty of his. He recommended that I remain in the back seat with him while his driver did the shopping.

As we waited I noticed a typical country newspaper editor with a green eyeshade, pencil over his ear, sleeve guards, and a sheaf of proof sheets in his hand, pause and, from the sidewalk, make an inventory of the big black limousine, the license number, and the passengers. He then hurried away up the street.

After a few minutes the editor returned, minus his editorial makeup, and under his arm he was carrying a generous crate of the most luscious-looking, pink-cheeked pears I had ever seen. He proudly presented them to us through the open window of the car as something by which to remember the prosperous little community. I accepted the crate of pears with thanks while the Chief sought to preserve his incognito.

But the fat was in the fire. From the large public school just across the street a horde of young folks, having finished their day's work, emerged and, seeing the editor standing by the window of the big black limousine, apparently surmised that some celebrity was in town. With screams of delight they descended on us, demanding autographs. Packed ten deep around the automobile, they passed in notebooks, textbooks, and scraps of wrapping paper for Mr. Hoover's signature. It was a bedlam. "Now look what you've done," said the Chief. "I haven't done a damned thing," said I, as the clamor for autographs continued and the crowds increased.

Then I saw a sweet-faced little old lady in a lace cap and shawl working her way through the crowds of school children. As she reached her lace-cuffed hand through the car window she smiled and said, "Is that really you, President Hoover? We all love you and I just want to go home and tell my family that I have seen you and shaken your hand."

In his embarrassment my great and good friend scarcely looked up, if at all, but he did take her by the hand for a moment.

The shouting of the school children had attracted a large assembly of the town folks by the time the chauffeur returned with the groceries. I waved to the crowd and we were off on the road again, leaving a group of shouting and waving citizens.

"Did you see that sweet little old lady, who only wanted to shake your hand?" I demanded.

"Yes," he replied.

"Well, you didn't act like it," I said. He hardly spoke to me the rest of the way to camp. After dinner each took his kerosene lamp and we all went to bed, with hardly a word spoken.

I didn't know whether the Chief was madder at me or the little editor or himself, but I knew things would be okay in the morning. They always had been.

The second incident occurred the following morning when we were up at dawn, assembling our fishing tackle by lamplight around the kitchen table, still in silence. It was just getting light when there came the sound of heavy footsteps on the porch and a shy knock at the door.

"See who that is, will you, Jay?" Mr. Hoover asked. A disheveled and ragged placer miner from a ramshackle cabin on the river had come for help. His daughter was very sick, he mumbled, and he was afraid maybe that she was dead. Was there someone here who could come and look at her?

Here was something the Chief was made for! He responded almost with a bound and, taking me with him, hastened to the miner's shack. It was a shambles of neglect.

The little girl had died of malnutrition and the rest of the children and the mother were in a pitiful state. There wasn't a scrap of food in the house, and the father was nearly incoherent from a steady diet of liquor.

Within an hour Mr. Hoover had learned the family history from the rural school teacher, had telephoned a rush order for supplies, and had a doctor and trained nurse on the way to the place. Characteristically, he then obtained enough contributions to set up a permanent organization in the little school district as a guarantee against a repetition of such an ugly tragedy.

By nine-thirty that forenoon every possible requirement had been arranged, and we went back to finish assembling our fishing tackle. For the rest of the day we were up to our hips in the tumbling current of the Rogue River.

The moral of these incidents, I think, is that Herbert Hoover never, to my knowledge, wanted anything for himself, but there was no limit to his energy and devotion if he could be of service to others. I never knew a man who could think and act so fast in the interest of any objective — except himself. Those who have not shared his personal friendship have missed a great privilege.

PART I

Food Administrator

Ding's devotion to all forms of conservation instinctively interested him in Herbert Hoover, newly appointed food administrator. Early evidence of Hoover's sound judgment, his ability to grasp and master seemingly impossible situations, and his unselfish devotion to his responsibilities were the qualities stressed by Ding which were to catch the attention and admiration of the American people. Hoover's long residence abroad, both as a mining engineer and as an administrator of relief in Europe, had prevented his participation in American public affairs, and he had no known political affiliation. His new popularity made him a political figure, and both parties were claiming him.

April 21, 1917

THIS WAS among the first cartoons to appear of the capable American Ding and others were beginning to admire. It was requested by, and given to, an associate of Hoover in the food administration. At this time Americans were reading the war news, and now and then stories of a different kind:

GERMANS ON VERGE OF REVOLT

HINDENBERG'S CONCENTRATION OF TROOPS GREATEST EVER KNOWN

British war cabinet calls into service every physician. . . . H. G. Wells recommends a form of government like that of the United States for Great Britain. . . . President Wilson reported ready to go before Congress to get "universal military service." . . . Earl Caddock of Walnut, Iowa, world champion wrestler, defeats Russian easily. . . . And hogs of 280 pounds sell at $16 per hundredweight.

It's going to be universal training for these, anyway.

May 24, 1917

THE UNITED STATES was in World War I and food was one of the allies' great problems at the time Ding put onto his drawing board the likeness of the man who was to "appear" there often in the next 15 years. The original of this was presented to Hoover. Austria was reported to be trying for peace with Russia, because of the food situation there. . . . A plan to pool allied purchasing was under consideration. . . . Headlines were saying:

MISSISSIPPI RIVER MAY BE UTILIZED FOR MOVEMENT OF GRAIN

PRES. WILSON SEEKS NEWS CENSORSHIP

HERBERT HOOVER OPENS NATIONAL FOOD ADMINISTRATION OFFICES

400 MILLIONS FOR ALLIES' JUNE LOAN

Getting rid of the family pet.

November 4, 1917

A MERICANS ACCEPTED the theory of food conservation, but were slow to practice it. The cartoon of this day was ringed on the front page by dramatic war news. The first Americans had been killed on the battlefields: Private Merle Hay of Glidden, Iowa, Private James Gresham of Evansville, Ind., and Private Thomas F. Enright of Pittsburgh, Pa. A headline said:

BRITISH SINK 12 HUN SHIPS

and a summary of war stories declared the Germans had withdrawn a few miles at Chemin-des-Dames. The National Coal Administration had granted the producers a 45-cent-a-ton increase in price to cover the wage boost given miners. . . . Premier Kerensky, representing the Bolsheviki who followed the Czar and preceded the communists, said Russia was growing tired of the war.

Can't you say something to him, Mr. Hoover?

January 1, 1918

S EVERAL CARTOONS about Hoover's food administration accomplishments dwelt on the way the women were co-operating in the effort to save foods. Here the imagination of the Ding pen produced some of its best work. Public interest at that period was centered on food, as the cartoon indicated, but other results of World War I were being reported, such as Germans trying to make separate peace deal with Russians. . . . McAdoo says food and coal shall be moved in transportation ahead of people. . . . British on sugar rations; first experience in food control.

UKRANIAN AND COSSACK FORCES ROUT BOLSKEVIKI

TURKS MASSACRE MILLION GREEKS

PEACE TALK CAUSES DROP IN CORN PRICE

The substitute on the water wagon route.

December 30, 1918

A YEAR PRIOR to Hoover's leaving Europe came this cartoon concerning the man who, by the same date a decade later, had been elected President, and was awaiting inauguration. In that final week of 1918 the major headlines read:

HUN TROOPS FIRE ON U.S. FLAG

FRENCH WON'T SEEK TERRITORY GAINS

IGNACE JAN PADEREWSKI ARRIVES IN POLAND TO FORM POST-WAR GOVERNMENT

Editorial comment was on President Wilson's speech in Guildhall, London. . . . On the sports pages Urban Shocker was taking his place with Ruth as a pitcher who could bat 300. . . . And on other pages Alexander Graham Bell declared against any government ownership of telephones.

Hoover will have to be careful or he'll be elected President.

March 12, 1919

EVEN DURING his food administration days,
before he was a cabinet member, Hoover was
handling foreign situations in a way that
won this pen-praise. Before Russia replaced
Bolshevism with communism, Hoover was
having a way with Bolshevism. The world
was then trying to recover from World War
I, but news could be personal if the person
was important enough. For instance, a headline said:

PRESIDENT WILSON'S COLD IMPROVES

Others read:

GERMANY BESET BY LOCAL CIVIL WAR

QUEEN MARIE TO VISIT U.S. SOON

**DRAFT OF PEACE TREATY NEARLY
COMPLETED**

**KAISER WILHELM ASKS PERMISSION TO MOVE
FROM HOLLAND BECAUSE OF HEALTH**

**FORMER PRESIDENT W. H. TAFT SPEAKS
AGAINST LEAGUE OF NATIONS**

Taming the wild ass.

January 29, 1920

THE SQUABBLE over Hoover's political affiliation so amused Ding that he produced this much-copied cartoon on that topic. Headlines of that day gave indications that the country was entering the Roaring Twenties:

BRYAN INSISTS THAT G.O.P. MAKE DECLARATION ON LIQUOR QUESTION

TENTATIVE RETURNS ON INCOME WON'T BE ALLOWED THIS YEAR

MANY RADIO EXPERTS INTERESTED IN MARS IDEA

CANADIAN PEOPLE URGED TO CHECK LAVISH SPENDING

And a nine-room modern home was advertised for $4,500.

One of those "party line" conversations.

February 15, 1920

THE SECOND CARTOON on Hoover's political affiliation was copied even more than the first one. Sharing the front pages with it were headlines and news stories such as:

PRES. WILSON PROMISES QUICK ADJUST-MENT OF RAILWAY WAGES

Mrs. Carrie Chapman Catt, president of the national League of Women Voters, urged women to work with the political parties. . . . Editorial comment was on President Wilson's dismissal of Secretary of State Lansing because he called cabinet meeting during the President's illness. . . . And a feature story read:

MARRIAGES CONTINUE IN HEAVEN, SAYS WIFE OF SIR OLIVER LODGE

One way to be sure of a good Sunday dinner.

PART II

Cabinet Member

Ding liked Hoover, the individual, and was intrigued by the tremendous tasks the remarkable public servant was assuming. Several of his well-known cartoons emphasized how very much the cabinet member was doing, and doing well. Others of this period reflected national concern over the trend toward moral laxity in private and public affairs. Hoover's unassailable record of integrity added to his prestige as an administrator, and Ding was quick to recognize that the people wanted leadership they could respect.

May 6, 1923

WHEN DING drew this cartoon, the first of his two Pulitzer prize-winners, the "Roaring Twenties" and the "Era of Prosperity" were in full swing. World news was prominent in the headlines:

FRENCH TRY KRUPPS PRESIDENT

PARIS REJECTS GERMAN PEACE PROPOSAL

U.S. CAN'T KEEP OUT OF EUROPE, HARDING WARNS

Other news stories featured events alarming to sober-minded people: 15-year-old "flappers" were found in raid on Chicago hop joint. . . . Marathon dancers were fainting after 90 hours continuous performance. . . . City vice squads were unable to cope with increased crime. . . . In the financial news:

FORD COMPANY TOPS WORLD IN CASH ON HAND

And 260-pound hogs bring $8.02 in Chicago.

AN ORPHAN AT 8 IS NOW ONE OF THE WORLD'S GREATEST MINING ENGINEERS AND ECONOMISTS WHOSE AMBITION IS TO ELIMINATE THE CYCLE OF DEPRESSION AND UNEMPLOYMENT

THE SON OF A PLASTERER IS NOW THE WORLD'S GREATEST NEUROLOGIST AND HIS HOBBY IS GOOD HEALTH FOR POOR CHILDREN

A PRINTER'S APPRENTICE IS NOW CHIEF EXECUTIVE OF THE UNITED STATES

BUT THEY DIDN'T GET THERE BY HANGING AROUND THE CORNER DRUG STORE

Good old U. S. A.

February 23, 1924

THE SCANDALS of the Harding administration, in which Hoover was Secretary of Commerce, emphasized by contrast the worth of the leaders *not* involved. The cartoon on this topic listed Hoover's name first, while the newspapers were saying that Bascom Slemp, secretary to President Coolidge, would be called as witness in the Senate oil inquiry. . . . General Smedley Butler told experiences as director of public safety of Philadelphia. . . . A committee in Congress approved a bill for $17,000,000 to improve the country's highways. . . . That day a federal judge dismissed the $200,000 libel suit against Henry Ford by Herman Bernstein, New York editor. . . . And Major F. L. Martin left Chicago for Los Angeles on the land leg of trip around the world by Army air squadron "world cruisers."

Thank goodness they're not all like that.

April 27, 1927

THE MULTITUDE of Hoover's in Washington traffic further amplified editorial interpretations of President Coolidge's statement that he was *not* considering Hoover for Secretary of State, should Kellogg retire. Commentators were trying to allay the fears of those who felt Hoover had too much power, that he was endangering the prestige of the President. Headlines featured the Mississippi River flood, with levees being cut to save New Orleans. . . . The movie industry had now become the 4th largest industry in the nation. . . . And sailors were injured by Chinese fire on a United States gunboat in the Yangtse River.

The traffic problem in Washington, D. C.

August 11, 1927

PRESIDENT COOLIDGE'S controversial statement of Aug. 2, "I do not choose to run" had unleashed mass speculation about whether he meant "No," or only "Maybe." And if he meant "No," who would be his successor? Some Midwesterners were pushing a Lowden-Dawes "twinship," but Ding felt Hoover was the favorite of the rank-and-file Republican. Headlines featured the Sacco-Vanzetti trial, with Charles Lindbergh and Aimee Semple McPherson sharing lesser space. . . . The smallest corn crop in 26 years forced December delivery price to a seasonal high of $1.18. . . . France was again hedging on war debts. . . . The 5-power naval conference at Geneva had collapsed. . . . And Babe Ruth hit his 36th home run.

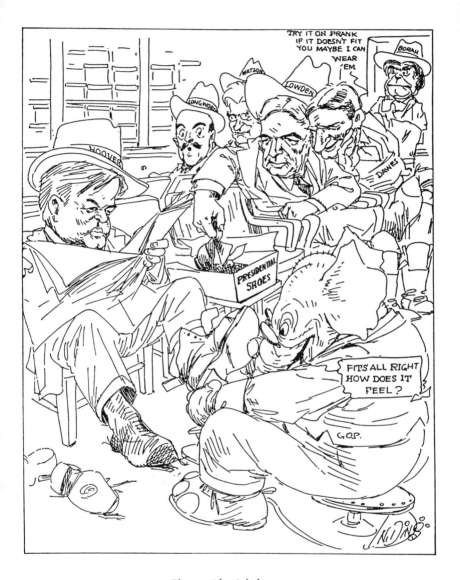

The presidential shoes.

September 21, 1927

EVEN WHEN HOOVER was being spoofed for his apparent indifference to the 1928 presidential nomination, he was shown working — which the others certainly were not. But politics was not all that concerned the people at that time. A Minnesota Senator predicted that Calvin Coolidge still would be the G.O.P. candidate. . . . Tunney (who held out for — and got — a 20-foot arena) and Dempsey were girding themselves for the "Title Bout of the Century" the following evening. . . . The leader in the National Air Derby had completed the New York–St. Paul leg in 9 hours, 9 minutes. . . . Dwight D. Morrow had been named Ambassador to Mexico — but a bitter fight loomed over this appointment from the J. P. Morgan firm. . . . And frost periled Iowa corn.

My word! What ardent lovers.

PART III

Candidate

Hoover's personal popularity was gaining such momentum that his recognition as the "people's choice" awaited only definite word from President Coolidge that he would not be a candidate. Defeat of the "Party Bosses" at the convention delighted Ding, for now Hoover could wage a campaign unrestricted by patronage promises.

November 22, 1927

DURING THE MONTHS before the 1928 convention, President Coolidge did not definitely clarify whether he would be a candidate, if drafted. As speculation continued, newspapers proclaimed:

SET MAXIMUM TAX SLASH AT 250 MILLIONS

TABER ELECTED TO HEAD GRANGE FOR 3RD TIME

GORDON PLANS "SURPRISE" IN FALL-SINCLAIR JURY QUIZ

ASK COOLIDGE TO INTERVENE IN COAL STRIKE

KEARNS-DEMPSEY TRIAL ENDS IN NONSUIT

Something seems to be holding them back.

December 29, 1927

Months ahead of the convention, the political situation as to Herbert Hoover led the party leaders (Ding called them bosses) to try to steer the party's thinking *away* from Hoover. Meantime:

U.S. PAYS TAX REBATES TO 240,000

read a headline; among the recipients were former President Taft, Harry Lauder, and Judge Kenesaw Mountain Landis. . . . Mexican Senate started action on the law which eventually took over U. S.-owned oil wells. . . . Colonel Charles Lindbergh was on a good-will trip to Central America. . . . Attempt was being made to reach an agreement with President Coolidge on McNary-Haugen farm bill, which he vetoed. . . . And

REPORT GEHRIG WANTS $25,000

the sports pages said.

One of those party line calls.

March 22, 1928

There came the time, then, when Hoover was generally recognized as the leading candidate for the nomination, but there were the usual "favorite sons" of several states who could be expected to have complimentary votes. Meantime, the first volume of the confidential messages of the United States government relating to the outbreak of World War I was issued by the state department. . . . A. B. Fall, Secretary of the Interior in the Harding administration and central figure in the oil scandals, thought near death, offered to "tell all" to the court scheduled to try him. . . . 22 countries against Russ disarmament plan. . . . Wilbur W. Marsh, treasurer of the national Democratic party, denies agreement with G.O.P. treasurer to withhold reports of contributions. . . . Sure strokes by Hennessy beat Tilden in Davis Cup trials. . . . Representative used-car offer — a 1927 Star for $275.

A lot of space for little boys who are going only to the first water tank.

June 13, 1928

THE "BIGGEST NEWS" of the day was, of
course, Hoover's assured new position as the
center of public attention. Other news was:
Farmers storm G.O.P. resolution committee — but the Haugen plank was rejected. . . .
Mabel Boll and Amelia Earhart, women
fliers, prepared to race at dawn from United
States to England. . . . Graham McNamee
announces G.O.P. national convention on
radio. . . . Iowa corn "far ahead of normal.". . .
The cabinet of German Chancellor William
Marx, Catholic party leader, resigns to President Hindenburg.

Just like that!

June 15, 1928

DING THEN SUMMED UP the convention: his friend as nominee, the professional politicians he so disliked scattered around debris-fashion, and, from out the Democratic dressing room, Governor Al Smith and the Democratic donkey — soon to be opposing Herbert Hoover and the elephant — peeking anxiously through the curtains.

Who said he wasn't a strong candidate?

June 16, 1928

TONGUE-IN-CHEEK, Ding penned Hoover with his baseball cap at a very un-Hooverish angle in the new "Republican Battery," with Senator Curtis as his teammate. Coolidge, weary from an arduous trip of many stops, was arriving at his summer White House at Cedar Island, Wisconsin. . . . Thirteen nations paid sums on their debt to the United States — a total of just over $90 million. . . . Babe Ruth was cracking out his 24th homer of the season!

Introducing the new battery.

July 23, 1928

MIDWAY IN THE SUMMER of the 1928 presidential campaign Hoover's many abilities were emphasized while readers were noting:

TWO AMERICANS RACE AROUND GLOBE IN 23 DAYS

WILL ROGERS CONCLUDES VISIT TO CAMP HEENEY

ENGLISH DANCE TEACHER ASSAILS MARATHON EVENTS

FRENCH PLANE TRYING TO SPAN ATLANTIC FROM EAST TO WEST

BERNARD SHAW FINALLY AGREES TO VISIT AMERICA

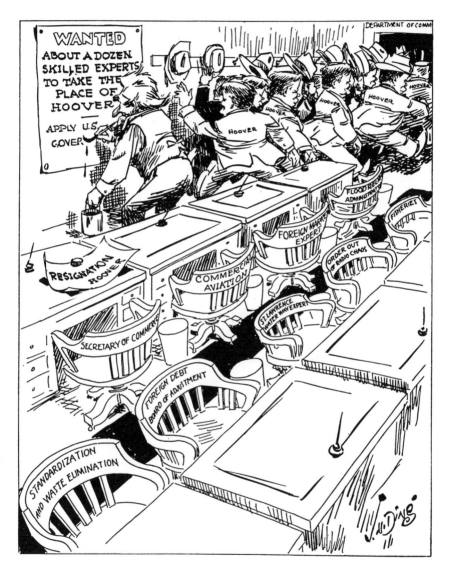

When Hoover turns in his resignation.

August 21, 1928

Iɴ Wᴇꜱᴛ Bʀᴀɴᴄʜ, Iᴏᴡᴀ, the only topic was the return of Herbert Hoover to his birthplace and boyhood home. Elsewhere in the world reporters were recording that:

SMITH BRANDS WILLIAM ALLEN WHITE CHARGES "UNFAIR"

ISSUE WARRANTS AGAINST TOM MIX FOR FIGHT

NAVY PERFECTS NEW MAGAZINE FOR EX- PLOSIVES

JIMMY WALKER GREETS ENGLISH WOMAN MAYOR

And a woman swimmer sets a new endurance record of 50 hours, 56 minutes, and 30 seconds.

As the twig is bent — the tree is inclined.

August 22, 1928

As MEANINGFUL as reporters' stories and photographers' pictures about Hoover's day in West Branch was the Ding's-eye-view. Meanwhile, divers were salvaging the sunken submarine S-4. . . . W. F. Whiting was named to succeed Hoover as Secretary of Commerce. . . . Helen Wills was polishing off a tournament foe in 22 minutes. . . . And the Redlegs stopped the Giants 3–2 in the pennant fight.

Homecoming day in West Branch.

November 7, 1928

ALTHOUGH HE NEVER doubted that Hoover would be elected, Ding drew a special cartoon for the newspapers' early editions on the evening of election day — editions that would be published before the final returns were in. This cartoon was replaced by another a few hours later. Mostly the headlines that day concerned politics, but there were a few other news stories. Republicans generally swept nation but Franklin Delano Roosevelt, Democrat, elected governor of New York and Ruth Bryan Owen, Democrat, daughter of W. J. Bryan, elected congresswoman from Florida. . . . Poincaré cabinet resigned in France, after two-year period in office. . . . Chicago top hog price, $9.80.

Neck and neck at the quarter pole.

November 10, 1928

THE WEEK FOLLOWING Hoover's election was filled with many stories about him and his plans. But there were other headlines. too.

HOOVER SOLEMN IN VICTORY

DARWINISM IS LOSING IN ARKANSAS VOTE

ROGERS HORNSBY SOLD TO CUBS

STRONG UPSWING OPENS "HOOVER" STOCK MARKET

And Byrd's expedition at South Pole thanks Iowa boys for sending football scores by radio.

An awful big contract.

PART IV

*P*resident

Hoover's election inspired Ding to interpret with deep sympathy the President's reticent personality and the immensity of his problems. Congressional lethargy and public unwillingness to face reality were the objects of many cartoon barbs, and as early as *1929*, Ding was apprehensive that these factors would obstruct the administration's program.

February 28, 1929

THE FACT THAT the new President was an engineer was in editorial — and cartoon — comment. The news of the week was varied: James Good of Iowa and W. D. Mitchell of Minnesota named by President Hoover to his cabinet. . . . Young Stribling of Georgia loses to Jack Sharkey by decision in heavyweight fight. . . . Charles Chaplin has 101-degree temperature as result of ptomaine poisoning. . . . Lindbergh and his future wife, Anne Morrow, crash in plane in Mexico; he protects her by wrapping her in cushions. . . . Report that Thomas D. Campbell, big-scale farmer of Montana, might be Secretary of Agriculture arouses speculation because he has just returned from study of Russian farming.

Fine opportunity for a modern engineer if they'll let him work.

March 4, 1929

HOOVER'S INAUGURATION was the big event of this day, but there also was news about revolution flaring in Mexico, with President Gil, former President Calles, and Generals Manzo and Topete as principal figures. . . . It was reported that Colonel Robert W. Stewart probably would not be re-elected board chairman of Standard Oil. . . . Massachusetts legislature voted for the second time in ten years not to repeal the vote of banishment voted on Roger Williams in *1635*. . . . President Hoover completed his cabinet by the appointment of Charles Francis Adams, member of the famous family, as Secretary of the Navy. . . . A headline read:

PRESIDENT AND MRS. COOLIDGE RETIRING FROM PUBLIC LIFE, RELATIVELY POOR

While such things are possible there is nothing very wrong with our country.

March 16, 1929

THE FIGURES of the oil scandals of the early 1920's came back into the news from time to time. This was the period of early aviation development — Captain Ira Eaker failed to make dawn-to-dusk flight from Tampico, Fla., to Brownsville, Tex. . . . Other news was: Libel trial of William McAndrew, former Chicago superintendent of schools, against Mayor William Hale Thompson is called. . . . Constance Bennett, actress, critically ill. . . . Byrd expedition at South Pole worries about failure of Bernt Balchen, Harold June, and Larry Gould to return from a trip to Rockefeller Mountain Range. . . . Senator Arthur Capper outlines the "essentials of a farm relief plan."

Putting 'em out of reach.

March 24, 1929

THE BIG NEWS of the first month of the new administration was made by President Hoover, of course. Other headlines were:

35 KILLED IN DIXIE STORMS

GRAF ZEPPELIN BEGINS ASIATIC JAUNT TONIGHT

HOW HENRY FORD DOES THE SQUARE DANCE

All Americans in Mexico City reported safe from fighting going on in revolution. . . . Cabinet members Wilbur and Mellon to speak on radio. . . . 300-mile trip across Canadian wilds begun on two tractors. . . . And a 1925 Buick sedan, offered at $450, was representative of used-car prices.

That's all right, Mr. President. We can just shake hands with ourselves.

March 28, 1929

S HORTLY AFTER HOOVER was inaugurated, there loomed, among his other problems, the difficult one of patronage. Meantime, with the administration getting on its way, there was other news: Bankers smash the money jam in New York. . . . Alf M. Landon, chairman of the Kansas State Republican Central Committee, suggested to succeed Vice-President Charles Curtis as Senator from Kansas. . . . Editorial comment on state scandals in Oklahoma recalled that, in twenty years, Oklahoma had impeached all but two of its governors. . . . Former President Coolidge wrote that "our national defense should be strong enough so that other nations would foresee a good deal of peril in attacking us."

STRONG HANDS PUT STOCKS ON UPWARD TRAIL

A long needed admonition.

April 12, 1929

THE SEEMINGLY EVER-PRESENT farm problem was demanding solution again. And, too, there was news about Marion Talley, Kansas farm girl who became youngest star of Metropolitan Opera company, then quit to go back to farm. . . . Other news included: What to do about liquor on steamship Leviathan plagues dry official. . . . Ruling on Illinois law means women must go to regular barber shops for hair cuts. . . . Jack Dempsey sued for $500,000 on claim he refused to fight Harry Wills. . . . Fred Hartley (later of Taft-Hartley labor-law fame) became baby member of House of Representatives.

Except in a purely advisory capacity the President expects to remain in the background.

May 12, 1929

A CARTOON which appeared in the press in the spring of 1929, stressed the factor that was to become the insurmountable obstacle to Hoover's program. Administration problems were making news, but there was other news, too: Discussion of higher tariff in United States arouses Europe. . . . Canadian forest fires spread near Winnipeg. . . . Government attack on plan of former Premier Lloyd George is feature of British general election. . . . Harry F. Sinclair, millionaire oil man in prison following oil scandals, loses right to tip penitentiary attendants. . . . "Sex," says Freud, "is the root and the fruit and the blossom of the Tree of Life."

Gulliver and the Lilliputians.

May 26, 1929

I N THE THIRD MONTH of Hoover's presidential administration, this cartoon asked a question that has been answered in the years since. That was 1929, and the world was making news like this: At Fort Worth, Tex., two fliers had stayed in the air 159 hours. . . . Mussolini emphasized in a speech the independence of the Italian kingdom and the Pope. . . . Mrs. Gene Tunney was very ill. . . . Investigations were under way which led to University of Iowa's ouster from the Western Athletic Conference. . . . Charles Lindbergh and Anne Morrow were planning their marriage for May 28.

How will Hoover go down in history?

January 29, 1930

LIQUOR SMUGGLING around the perimeter of the nation had emphasized the "prohibition question," and the clamor for action offered Congress another opportunity to delay decisions on much-needed domestic and foreign legislation. Italian Foreign Secretary Grandi was shouting for action at the London five-nation naval conference. . . . Premier de Rivera of Spain dramatically resigned. . . . Army and Navy Journal editorially opposed appointments of inspector general and quarter master general. . . . But John Q. Citizen found relief from heavy news in:

DEMPSEY COLORFUL IN REFEREEING

While the family dinner gets cold.

February 13, 1930

IN THE VITAL YEARS of his administration, President Hoover and the Senate often disagreed, which probably made the President's fishing trips more enjoyable. "Frazzled-nerved" senators were delaying tariff action. . . . Senator Borah condemned Hoover's selection of Charles Evans Hughes as Chief Justice. . . . Senator Heflin indignantly denied (in *Congressional Record*) his use of a hand gesture to imply Senator Copeland would be lynched if he came into the South. . . . Five-power naval conference failed to abolish submarine warfare. . . . Agricultural papers demanded the United States withdraw from the Philippines.

G.O.P. CHIEF QUIZZED ON MUSCLE SHOALS LOBBYING

GRAIN STABILIZATION CORPS BUYS WHEAT

And Richard Dix was tugging heartstrings in theaters across the nation.

Why presidents go a-fishing.

April 5, 1930

W HEN THE WORLD depression began to affect the United States heavily in 1929 and 1930, President Hoover began pouring federal money into public construction to aid the nation's economy. This was seen as a "priming of the pump," and the phrase became a part of the American business language. Top headlines on that day were mostly about foreign affairs, including:

GANDHI MAKES SALT FROM SEA

London parley of United States, England, France, Italy, and Japan on naval security was near break-up. . . . France passes Young Plan for handling reparations payments from Germany, as result of World War I. . . . And the Senate votes to turn Muscle Shoals nitrate plant to government-controlled corporation to study fertilizer production.

Priming the old pump.

July 19, 1930

MIDWAY THROUGH the administration of President Hoover, a sympathetic and light-hearted cartoon appeared. There were items of news other than administrative on the front pages that day: Turk, aged 156 years, never has tasted intoxicating liquor, he says. Some of the headlines were:

STERILIZATION PROBLEMS FACE SOCIAL WORKERS

FORMER KAISER LIVES QUIETLY AT HIS HOME AT DOORN, HOLLAND

IOWA RANKS AS GREATEST ROAD-BUILDER IN U.S. WITH $38,000,000 FOR 1930

And a London treaty limiting all classes of ships in American, British, and Japanese navies is ratified by United States Senate.

The President's nice restful vacation trip.

October 4, 1930

THE DIRECTNESS and vigor with which Hoover did his work featured today's cartoon, and with it came this variety of news stories: Clark of Utah named ambassador to Mexico. . . . Chicago investigating slaying of Jake Lingle, newspaperman pal of gangsters.

LEGION EXPECTED TO SEEK SHOW-DOWN ON LIQUOR

"Communist" parade of 600, on way to hall where President Hoover was speaking in Cleveland, is broken up. . . . Henry Ford predicts in a book that, by 1950, daily wage of American worker will be $27.

The American doughboy was never like this.

January 23, 1931

AFTER TWO YEARS of Hoover's administration, there was little if any doubt that he would be renominated by his party, and there was no doubt that the party's platform would have in it a dry plank. Meantime, the people were reading:

PAVLOVA IS DEAD AT AGE 45

WETS WHIPPED IN ATTACK IN CONGRESS ON DRY FUND

GRAPEFRUIT THROWN AT RUDY VALLEE

GANDHI OUTLINES PLANS TO DISCUSS INDIAN FREEDOM WITH BRITISH

VALIDITY OF NEBRASKA LAW GUARANTEEING BANK DEPOSITS INTO U. S. SUPREME COURT

Nailing down the first plank in the 1932 platform.

May 7, 1931

L AMENTABLE ECONOMIC CONDITIONS of Europe were dragging down the United States and, as if that were not enough, those countries were pleading with United States for aid. But not all was foreign news.

TROOPS RUSH TO KENTUCKY MINES

RUSSIA TAKES PLACE AS WHEAT-PRODUCING KING

Baltimore & Ohio Railroad announces first entirely air-conditioned train. . . . Father Charles E. Coughlin is called "America's father confessor of the air." . . . Mark Sullivan writes from Washington that cancellation of the debts of the European nations to United States is unlikely.

Where most of it goes.

October 27, 1931

WHEN AMERICAN BUSINESS was weakening against the world's bad economic conditions, Hoover, as President, arranged a half-billion-dollar credit. In that same period: Germany was trying for reopening of reparations question. . . . Governor Franklin Roosevelt of New York criticized Al Smith in speech. . . . Army football player Richard Sheridan died as a result of broken neck, sustained in Army–Yale game.

LANDSLIDE FOR MACDONALD FORCES IN BRITISH ELECTION

. . . And Chicago wheat price was 57½ cents a bushel.

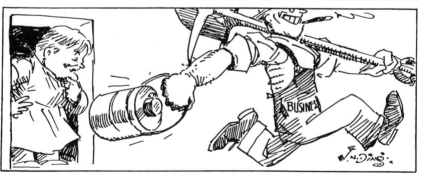

A new backbone seemed to be what was needed.

November 23, 1931

T HERE WERE TIMES, however, when the well-known Ding humor portrayed Hoover in amusing situations. This was the time, too, when:

DEMOCRATIC NATIONAL CHAIRMAN TO POLL PARTY ON LIQUOR

RUSSIAN PRESS SEES "CAPITALISTIC" ATTEMPT TO EMBROIL THAT NATION IN MANCHURIA

Tulane, Southern California, and Northwestern were leading contenders as national football champs. . . . And Secretary of Labor Doak was at work after illness.

A tough customer to please.

December 2, 1931

ALWAYS THERE ARE many persons and organizations advising the President what to do. This was especially true in 1931 when President Hoover was trying to guide the United States through the world-wide series of economic and governmental crises. Flanking the front page cartoon on this topic that day were:

COMMUNISTS STAGE SCENE AS CONGRESS CONVENES

MAYOR JIMMY WALKER PLEADS "FREE MOONEY"

HOOVER'S RECOVERY PROGRAM BEFORE CONGRESS

METROPOLITAN PLAYS FIRST TIME IN SUBURBS

RIOTING IN CUBA CAUSES DEATHS

NEW AUSTRIAN CABINET FORMED

Bridge Whist isn't the only game that has kibitzers.

December 18, 1931

IN THE LATTER MONTHS of 1931 the awful problems of the world depression dominated American affairs. . . . Congress began considering Hoover Plan for war debt cancellation. . . . Farm board says hog prices too low, cites figure of $4.18 a hundredweight compared to $7.92 year before.

JOBLESS RELIEF DRIVE LAUNCHED IN IOWA

RAILROADS PLAN 15 PERCENT WAGE CUT

But among the lighter headlines:

DAMON RUNYON DETECTS WHITE HAIR IN DEMPSEY'S CROWN

Of course we are all keeping our heads and doing all we can to help.

January 6, 1932

There were times in 1931 and 1932 when the relations of President Hoover and the Democratic Congress were very much in the public considerations. The public was also hearing about:

NEW HAMPSHIRE WET IS VICTOR

Half million dollars stolen from Lincoln, Nebr., bank is returned. . . . Lieutenant Alfred M. Gruenther, who refereed bridge contest in which Ely Culbertson played, writes articles for press on contest. . . . Writer says "Sweden is full of Garbos." . . . Eleven thousand unemployed marchers, en route to Washington, are at Huntington, W. Va.

The special message.

January 18, 1932

SEVERAL OF THE CARTOONS concerning
Hoover's methods of meeting the world depression evidenced what friends of the cartoonist knew — that Ding's boyhood ambition
was to be a doctor. Along with this medical
scene appeared these news stories:

END OF OPEN DOOR SEEN IN FAR EAST ROW

David Lloyd George, British war-time Premier, is feted on 69th birthday. . . . Congress
begins conferences on establishment of Reconstruction Finance Corporation and re-
capitalization of Federal Land Banks. . . .
Theodore Dreiser completes book flaying
capitalistic system. . . . Funeral services held
for former Queen Sophie of Greece, sister of
Kaiser Wilhelm.

The new antitoxin.

May 1, 1932

THE FUSSING between the wet and dry factions of the Republican party was on the editorial pages. On the front pages were these stories: Reparations, war debts, and disarmament are issues in French election. . . . Army tests .276 Garand rapid-fire rifle. . . . Barbara Hutton, "New York society girl," to lead pageant at New York charity ball. . . . Democratic leaders study April primaries as showing strength of Governor Franklin Roosevelt and former Governor Al Smith, aspirants for the Democratic presidential nomination. . . . Crop estimates show huge abandonment of winter wheat acreage. . . . Sixteen world records smashed at Drake relays.

Well, they can't stand there.

May 13, 1932

IN THE LATTER two years of his administration, Hoover often did not have the co-operation of Congress. This situation was discussed on the editorial pages, made news, and, of course, received the attention of Ding. The period was filled with other news, too.

LINDY BABY MURDERED; BODY FOUND NEAR HOME; DEAD TWO MONTHS

Vice President Curtis orders Senator Huey Long to sit down, during attack on Senator Robinson. . . . Government bond market reacts to proposals for two-billion-dollar relief expenditure. . . . Mother denies that 19-year-old Doris Duke, "world's richest girl," is engaged to a Mr. Quinn. . . . Probe of activities made following suicide of "match king" Ivan Kreuger shows many Americans lost fortunes.

If he'd cut it when he should it would all be done by this time.

June 13, 1932

By convention time in 1932, it was evident that Hoover and his administration would command the convention. Meantime: Iowa Amana colonies like corporation operation, ending 85 years of "communistic life." . . . Lindbergh kidnapping clue collapses. . . . Bonus marchers expect to have 15,000 at Washington in another day. . . . Prospects of Governor Franklin Roosevelt for Democratic presidential nomination increase. . . . Senator Dickinson of Iowa keynoter at Republican national convention at Chicago, which will open in two days. . . . Chicago corn price 30 cents a bushel, hogs $2.85.

The probable outcome.

July 13, 1932

IN 1932 the nation had a Republican President and a Democratic Congress. Ding favored the re-election of Hoover, and in a midsummer cartoon he summed up his views. Bounding this were such news stories as: Libby Holman Smith, torch singer, leaves for New York after funeral of her husband of six weeks, Reynolds Smith, tobacco heir.

SENATE PASSES HOME LOAN BILL

AMELIA EARHART TRIES TRANS-CONTINENTAL NON-STOP RECORD FLIGHT

DE VALERA OF IRELAND STILL TWISTING LION'S TAIL

The delayed nourishment.

August 12, 1932

By MID-AUGUST the presidential campaign was developing its strength, and the major news stories, headlines, and cartoons dealt with its aspects. Ding provided one of his best. Other — perhaps lesser — news included: Mayor Jimmy Walker of New York City pleads with Governor Roosevelt to keep his job, despite scandal. . . . Jean Harlow heads group of actors and actresses supporting Governor Roosevelt for president. . . . Mrs. Ida B. Wise-Smith of Iowa expected to be elected national head of W.C.T.U. at convention.

U.S. HUNTS KEY TO SOVIET TRADE

Billy Sunday's own story of his life is being serialized in a national magazine.

A message to the home folks.

October 4, 1932

CAMPAIGNING FOR RE-ELECTION, Hoover came to Iowa for a major address. Ding, living in Des Moines, made his cartoon especially pertinent to the home state of the President. Hoover was all the news Iowa wanted that day, but elsewhere there were headlines on other topics: Rear Admiral Richard Byrd denounced the bonus payment plan. . . . The National Farm Holiday Association announced plan to parade in Des Moines in protest against low farm prices. . . . Reported that franchise of St. Louis Cardinals would be transferred to Montreal. . . . Stock transactions at New York fell below one million shares in dullest market since July 21.

Surely these two overburdened men ought to be able to understand each other.

October 17, 1932

THE AUTUMN of 1932 was a period of national political campaigning. What Hoover had done to bolster his country against the world's depression was under fire by his political opponents. A crowd of 25,000 stood in the rain and cheered Mussolini, pleading for "bloodiest modern revolution."

WORLD TRADE BARRIERS DRAW IRE OF VON PAPEN, GERMAN CHANCELLOR

HINT AT WORLD SCANDAL OVER INSULL PROBE

BRAIN TRUST HELPING GOV. ROOSEVELT WRITE SPEECH

Alice Roosevelt Longworth, daughter of Theodore Roosevelt, wrote that Franklin Delano Roosevelt was only a distant relative of hers.

We'd have found out if we hadn't had 'em.

November 3, 1932

ANGERED AND ANGUISHED by the unwarranted abuse heaped upon the President, Ding drew this poignant cartoon of his friend — a tribute to his achievements, and a prophecy of future recognition of the essential greatness of the man. Extravagant campaign reporting was intermingled with ominous news: Europe was torn with labor riots and crumbling economies. . . . English idle were marching on Parliament. . . . 15,000 hungry idle were shouting "Vote Red" as they paraded in Chicago. . . . City agencies were coordinating and increasing relief activities. . . . Educators were predicting complete state support for all public schools. . . . In the financial field: General Motors pays dividend despite slump . . . but beef was ranging from $6 to $8, with highest corn futures barely reaching thirty cents. . . . And *The Literary Digest,* most conservative of all polls, predicted Roosevelt would carry 41 states.

The U. S. award for distinguished service.

PART V

Post-Presidential Years

The friendship between Ding Darling and Herbert Hoover grew stronger after Hoover's presidency. For nearly thirty years, the two men wrote regularly to each other on a variety of issues. Their periodic fishing trips gave them the opportunity to share their love of the outdoors and to hunt for the elusive brook trout!

Ding continued to draw Hoover in the 1930s and 1940s as warranted by events. For the most part, he depicted Hoover as the leader of the loyal opposition, fighting against the New Deal policies of Franklin D. Roosevelt. But above all else, Ding was proudest of his friendship with Herbert Hoover, a feeling he captured in the 1955 cartoon that closes this edition.

NOVEMBER 26, 1935—Would Hoover run for the presidency in 1936? Ding helped to clarify the former president's intentions in this *Des Moines Register* cartoon. "Not a candidate," noted the caption, "just a coach." Judging by the expression on Hoover's face, he was none too happy with the crowd of potential candidates to run against Roosevelt. The nomination was eventually won by Alf Landon of Kansas. We can only wonder what is going on in the mind of Senator William E. Borah of Idaho.

New Dealers Didn't Like Hoover's Speech

JUNE 28, 1944—Herbert Hoover was in a combative mood as he prepared to address the Republican national convention in 1944. "I am going to stay in this fight until I die," Hoover said in reference to the Republican assault on Roosevelt and his New Deal policies. And Hoover was true to his word in his speech on June 27. Ding was among the many Americans cheering Hoover on. In a cartoon published in the *Chicago Tribune* on June 28, Ding showed a vigorous Hoover knocking out the Democrats. A scowling Roosevelt was left to clean up the mess.

OCTOBER, 1955—In addition to winning two Pulitzer prizes, Ding also received a second "Iowa Award," the state's highest honor. Created at the time of the state centennial in 1946, the Iowa Award was presented first to Herbert Hoover in 1951. Ding received his award four years later, generating a congratulatory letter from Hoover. "There is no greater tribute that can come from the people of Iowa," Hoover wrote on September 25, "and no one deserves it so greatly as you." Ding responded with this undated drawing, to which Hoover replied in jest: "I do not weigh quite so much as you think."